GREECE

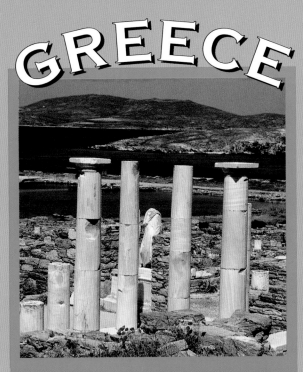

A TRUE BOOK

by

Christine Petersen and
David Petersen

Children's Press®

A Division of Scholastic Inc.

New York Toronto London Auckland Sydney
Mexico City New Delhi Hong Kong
Danbury, Connecticut

Traditional Greek clothing

Reading Consultant
Linda Cornwell
*Coordinator of School Quality
and Professional Improvement
Indiana State Teachers
Association*

Library of Congress Cataloging-in-Publication Data

Petersen, Christine, 1965–
    Greece / by Christine Petersen and David Petersen.
        p. cm. — (A true book)
    Includes bibliographical references and index.
    ISBN 0-516-22255-4 (lib. bdg.)   0-516-27359-0 (pbk.)
    1. Greece—Juvenile literature. [1. Greece.] I. Petersen, Christine.
II. Title. III. Series.
    DF717 .P48 2001
    949.5—dc21   00-064385

©2001 Children's Press®
A Division of Scholastic Inc.
Printed in China.
6 7 8 9 10 R 14 13 12

Contents

Something Old, Something New

Greece is special in at least three ways. First, one of the oldest civilizations on the European continent was born in Greece. Second, Greece is the most southern country in Europe. Third, Greece is really two countries in one—a combination of old and new.

Athens is Greece's seaside capital city. It has high-rise apartments, churches, schools, and people everywhere.

Athens, Greece's capital city, has a mix of ancient and modern buildings.

Like many cities, Athens is heavily polluted.

It also has cars and noise and smog. Athens seems a lot like any big city—until you look up.

The Parthenon (above), perched on the Acropolis, is a reminder of Greece's glorious past. As many as thirty teams of oxen hauled each large piece of stone for the Parthenon's columns (right).

Right in the middle of the hustle and bustle, on a flat-topped hill called the Acropolis, stands a huge stone building called the Parthenon. This structure was built almost 2,500 years ago, during the proudest days of ancient Greece. It is known for its rows of high columns.

Where in the World Is Greece?

On a map, Greece looks like a human hand with long, crooked fingers reaching into the sea. Away from the rocky coastline, the land rises and falls like waves. Blue mountain ranges separate green plains and valleys.

A quiet valley town
nestled below mountains

Greece is a small country,
larger than New York State
but smaller than Florida. The
mainland extends fewer than
400 miles (644 kilometers) in

any direction. In Greece, you are never more than 85 miles (137 km) from the sea. Barely 51,000 square miles (132,000 square km) in size, this tiny country has a population of almost eleven million people.

Three countries form Greece's northern border: Albania, Macedonia, and Bulgaria. In its northeastern corner, Greece touches Turkey.

Greece has hundreds of islands, sprinkled like diamonds

Hundreds of islands are sprinkled along the coast of Greece.

across three seas: the Aegean Sea to the east, the Ionian Sea to the west, and the Mediterranean Sea to the south. The Greek Isles are a

Like Athens, this popular tourist town on the island of Rhodes has an acropolis high on a hill.

vacation paradise of quiet fishing villages and lovely beaches.

The highest point in Greece is Mount Olympus, rising 9,570 feet (2,917 meters) above the surrounding seas. Its peak is often frosted with snow or hidden in clouds. To the ancient Greeks, Mount Olympus was the home of Zeus and eleven lesser gods and goddesses.

Zeus, king of the Greek gods

Crete

Ruins along the coast of Crete

Crete is the largest of the Greek Isles. Beginning about five thousand years ago, a people called the Minoans lived there. They built grand palaces and practiced a sport similar to bullfighting.

In this mosaic, the warrior Theseus fights the legendary Minotaur.

According to legend, a man-eating monster called the Minotaur terrorized ancient Crete. Today, Crete has more than a million residents—no gods or monsters, but lots of fishers and farmers.

Fishing boats line this busy harbor.

The Glory of Ancient Greece

People have lived on the Balkan Peninsula, the land that is now Greece, for at least eight thousand years. About 3,600 years ago, a Balkan people called the Mycenaeans created the Greek language. An inventive and warlike culture, the Mycenaeans controlled the Mediterranean

This vase depicting Mycenaean warriors dates from around 1150 B.C.

Sea with warships and swords of bronze.

Ancient Greece's most famous period, the "Golden" (or Classical) Age, began about

A Classical Greek sculpture, carved out of marble

2,500 years ago. During this period, the ancient Greeks built the Parthenon and other beautiful buildings. They also carved huge statues from marble, a hard stone that can be polished. Today, Classical Greek architecture and art can be found everywhere.

The ancient Greeks developed *philosophy*, which means "love of knowledge" in Greek. Their philosophers were wise people and teachers who questioned the old beliefs in gods and monsters. They used science and reason to explore the mysteries

Socrates, famous philosopher of ancient Greece

of life and nature. Some of the most famous Greek philosophers were Socrates, Aristotle, and Sophocles.

Ancient Greece was also the birthplace of democracy, which comes from the Greek word *demokratia,* meaning "rule of the people." Rather than being told what to do by rulers or priests, many ancient Greeks chose their own leaders. Today, the United States and Greece are both democracies.

One of Greece's major historical figures was Alexander the Great, who became king

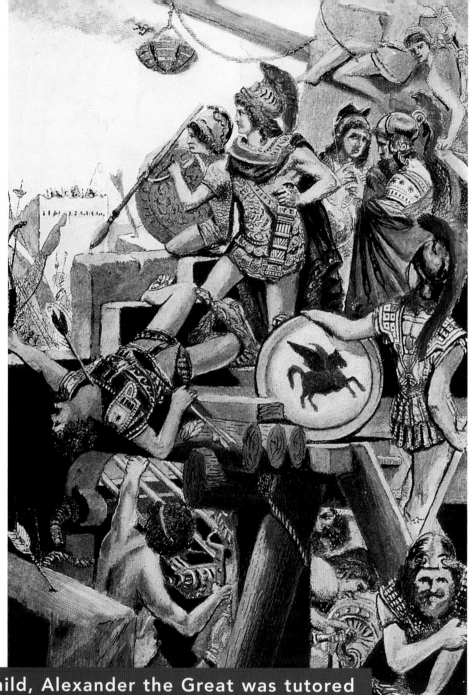

As a child, Alexander the Great was tutored by the great philosopher Aristotle. Here, he is victorious at the siege of Tyre in 332 B.C.

of Greece in 336 B.C. (Before Christ). As captain general of the Greek army, Alexander conquered a huge area of land from Greece to India. After Alexander's death, his generals divided up the empire. For the next two thousand years, Greece was ruled by Rome, Turkey, and other foreign powers. In 1830, Greece finally became an independent country again.

The Olympic Games

Ancient Olympians were crowned with wreaths of laurel, not medals of gold.

Beginning in 776 B.C., Greek athletes came from far and wide to a valley called Olympia. To honor the god Zeus, the athletes competed in wrestling, jumping, chariot racing, and other sports.

Today, the Olympic Games—Summer and Winter—are each held in a different country every four years. The games still begin at Olympia, though, with the lighting of the Olympic flame. The torch is carried to the host city by relay runners and by plane. Then an Olympic athlete is chosen to light the official torch to begin another Olympic Games.

Greek actresses light the Olympic torch using the sun's rays at the sanctuary of Olympia. This flame began the 1996 Summer Games in Atlanta, Georgia.

Modern Life and Culture

Modern Greece is governed by a president and a 300-member parliament, which makes the laws. Greece is not a wealthy country, but it has good schools, a rich culture, and a low crime rate.

Today, one-third of the Greek people live in or near the capital of Athens. The rest of the people

The Greek parliament building (above). A Greek girl takes care of her sister.

This farmer plows his fields with the help of a horse.

are spread among hundreds of farming and fishing villages. In some parts of Greece, especially the islands, people use more horse-drawn carts than cars.

People around the world agree that most Greek food is delicious. Lamb, fish, and spinach are favorite foods. Feta, or goat cheese, is served at many meals, and so are olives and garlic.

Greeks are known to be friendly, social people who

Greek people relaxing over dinner (above). *Baklava* (right) is a popular and delicious dessert.

enjoy getting together for dinner. One common group meal is *souvlakia*—Greek shish kebab. It is made by threading chunks of meat and vegetables onto a stick and roasting it over a fire. *Baklava,* a pastry made with honey and nuts, is a popular dessert.

In Greece, weddings and holidays always mean parties and feasting. An important national holiday is March 25, Greek Independence Day—much like the American Fourth of July. The biggest Greek holiday of all is Easter, celebrated everywhere in carnivals with dancing, music, and church ceremonies.

A musician plays the *zournas* as carnival dancers celebrate Easter in the northern town of Naousa.

No Greek festivity is complete without live music. Folk musicians still play instruments invented centuries ago, such as the *zournas*, a wind instrument like an oboe. The *bouzouki,* another traditional instrument, looks like a pot-bellied guitar. Modern music—from symphony orchestras to rock and roll—is popular in Greek cities.

Music from this man's *bouzouki* entertains people at the farmer's market.

Greek children start playing soccer at a very young age.

The Greek national sport is soccer, or *podosphero* (football). Many children begin playing soccer almost as soon

The Greek national soccer team plays against Denmark in a 1997 World Cup game.

as they can walk. The Greek national soccer team competes worldwide. Basketball is also very popular today, especially in schools.

Education and Employment

In the past, many people in Greece were not literate—they could not read or write. Today, nearly all grown-ups (95 percent) in Greece can read and write. Greek children now attend school from age six to fifteen. All education is free.

These schoolchildren in Gythium have a beautiful setting for their morning exercises.

After finishing school, many young people take jobs in the cities. Others make their living by fishing and farming. Ocean shipping is also a major indus-try in Greece. Many young

A father, son, and donkey team prepare to gather grapes.

Greeks become sailors and travel the world.

Greece has a mild climate and a long growing season. Important crops include beets, grains, olives, and grapes grown

Sheep grazing under an olive tree

for making wine. Just as in ancient times, sheep and goats roam Greece's rolling hills, providing milk, wool, and meat.

The scenic beauty of Greece, along with its fascinating history,

A cruise ship carries tourists through the Corinth Canal.

makes tourism its most important
business. Every year, millions of
visitors come to Greece and its
enchanting islands. Many tourists
come for the beaches, the food,
and the friendly people. They
also come to see the Parthenon

and other reminders of Greece's golden past. Few other countries can offer the striking blend of the ancient and the modern that is Greece.

Greek church overlooking the sea

To Find Out More

Here are some additional resources to help you learn more about the nation of Greece:

 Books

Allard, Denise. **Greece.** Raintree Steck-Vaughn Publishers, 1997.

Freeman, Charles. **The Ancient Greeks.** Oxford University Press, 1996.

Green, Robert. **Alexander the Great.** Franklin Watts, 1996.

Nardo, Don. **Life in Ancient Athens.** Lucent Books, 2000.

Rockwell, Anne. **The Robber Baby: Stories from the Greek Myths.** Greenwillow Books, 1994.

Shuter, Jane. **Farmers & Fighters.** Heinemann Library, 1999.

Organizations and Online Sites

Voyage Back in Time: Ancient Greece and Rome
http://www.richmond.edu/ ~ed344/webunits/ greecerome/

An introduction to ancient Greece and Rome.

Mythweb
http://www.mythweb.com

A great place to get to know the gods, heroes, and stories of ancient Greek mythology.

Elysium
http://library.thinkquest.org/ 26264/

Interactive website with good reviews of the characters, myths, and art of ancient Greece.

The Travel Channel Online
http://travel.discovery.com/ dest/lpdb/euro/grec/intro. html

Get the background on Greece's past and present, and enjoy a 360-degree webcam video of the Parthenon.

Important Words

architecture the design and construction of buildings

civilization a highly developed society

column a tall pillar that supports a building or statue

conquer to take control by force

democracy a government in which people choose their leaders

parliament the part of a country's government that makes the laws

peninsula a piece of land surrounded by water on three sides

reason powerful thinking and good judgment

ruins the remains of a building or other structure

Index

(**Boldface** page numbers indicate illustrations.)

Meet the Authors

Christine Petersen grew up near the Pacific Ocean in California. She now lives in the lake country near Minneapolis, Minnesota. Christine is a biologist, educator, and expert on North American bats. She enjoys hiking, snowshoeing, reading, travel, and playing with her two cats.

David Petersen is Christine's father. David lives in a self-built cabin in the San Juan Mountains of Colorado. He has been writing True Books for more than twenty years, and knows that nature is life's greatest gift.